CONTENTS

INTRODUCING . . .

MR ROBINSON

FRANZ

ERNEST

JUNO

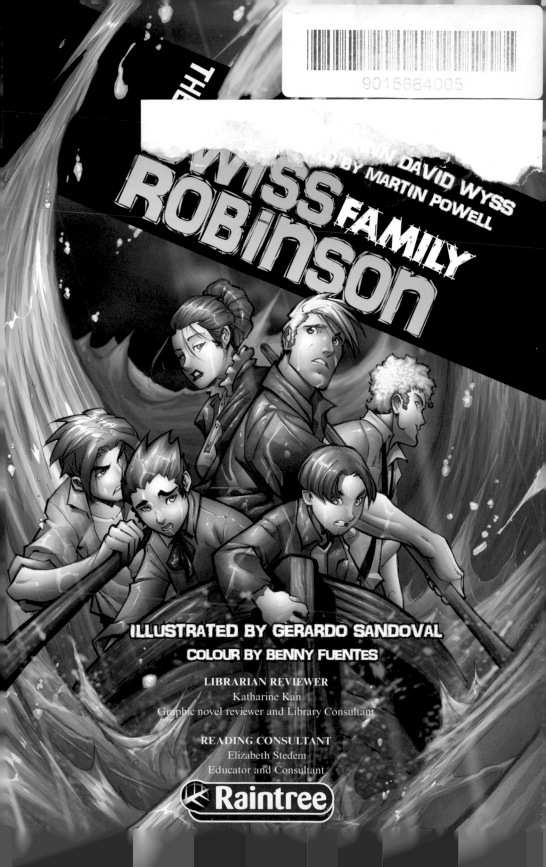

www.raintreepublishers.co.uk
Visit our website to find out
more information about
Raintree books.

To order:
☎ Phone 0845 6044371
🖷 Fax +44 (0) 1865 312263
📠 Email myorders@raintreepublishers.co.uk

Customers from outside the UK please telephone +44 1865 312262

Raintree is an imprint of Capstone Global Library Limited, a company incorporated
in England and Wales having its registered office at 7 Pilgrim Street, London, EC4V 6LB –
Registered company number: 6695582

Art Director: Heather Kindseth
Graphic Designer: Kay Fraser
Editor: Laura Knowles
Originated by Capstone Global Library Ltd
Printed and bound in China by Leo Paper Products Ltd

ISBN 978 1 406 22492 4 (hardback)
15 14 13 12 11
10 9 8 7 6 5 4 3 2 1

ISBN 978 1 406 22498 6 (paperback)
15 14 13 12 11
10 9 8 7 6 5 4 3 2 1

British Library Cataloguing in Publication Data
A full catalogue record for this book is available from the British Library.

FRITZ

TURK

JACK

MRS ROBINSON

In the early 19th century, my family and I set sail. We left our home in Switzerland to settle as missionaries in Australia.

CHAPTER 1

SHIPWRECKED!

But shortly into our voyage . . .

For six days and nights we were helplessly tossed in the sea. All hope was lost.

The captain and the crew escaped into the lifeboats, leaving my family to our fate.

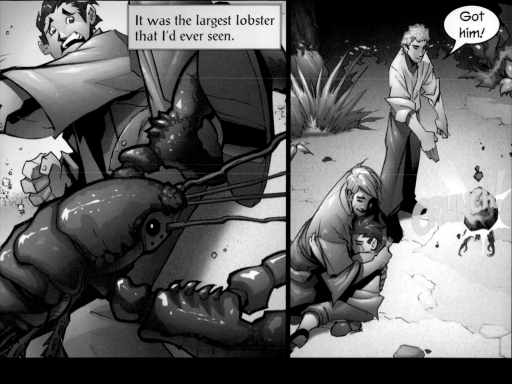

Back on the beach . . .

Look, Father! Franz and I made fishing poles!

Very clever! I see you already put them to good use!

This coconut milk is very tasty.

Drink your fill. Coconut trees abound here.

Tomorrow we'll search for a fresh water supply.

First, we'll return to the shipwreck.

We're going back on a rescue mission.

15

On shore . . .

Oh, my! What a frightful explosion!

And how clever!

Jack, Franz, you have the most ingenious father alive!

Turk?

What is it? Why are you growling, boy?

Row for shore quickly! I don't know how long those old barrels will keep the big animals afloat!

Oh, no!

SHARKS!

The first of many blessed miracles to come.

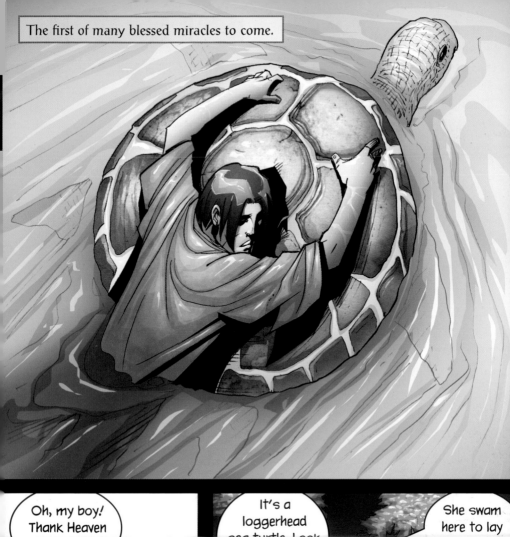

Oh, my boy! Thank Heaven you're safe!

It's a loggerhead sea turtle. Look at the size of her!

She swam here to lay her eggs!

19

20

The mystery of the vanished sheep continued to puzzle me. I could think of no earthly reason for its disappearance.

I kept the others busy, so they wouldn't be likely to worry themselves. They made pens for the animals, and a tent.

We would search for a new home tomorrow. The sooner the better.

I no longer felt safe there.

The next morning gave us new hope.

It is all so beautiful!

Yes, our own Garden of Eden.

CHAPTER 2
BUILDING A NEW HOME

She'd better not get too close to that porcupine!

BARK!

Juno, come back!

Jack! No!

It's so dark in here. I'll never find her.

Suddenly . . .

Materials from the shipwreck gave us timber, rope, nails, cloth, and even vegetable seeds for our garden.

At their mother's suggestion, the boys and I built our new home high amongst the branches.

Finally, after many months, our palace in the treetops was finished.

Isn't this a bit dangerous? For the children, I mean.

You're doing fine, my dear. Just don't look down.

Well, here we are. Welcome to Falconhurst, Mother!

It's even more beautiful than I dreamed!

27

The next day, we continued to explore.

Hmm. Looks like we're not the only hunters in the neighbourhood. We'd better move on.

Quickly.

The more we explored, the more surprised we became with the animal life surrounding us.

My knowledge of the subject was challenged almost daily.

The plants, too, were like nothing I had ever seen.

This is a great discovery! Unless I'm mistaken, it's a manioc root! We can make flour with this!

That means we can have bread!

Yes, now where did those boys run off to?

Father! Mother!

Run for your lives!!

Cape buffalo were the most dangerous beasts of the jungle. The trees were the only safe place from them.

Your own personal stairwell, m'lady.

You'll never need to fear that ladder again.

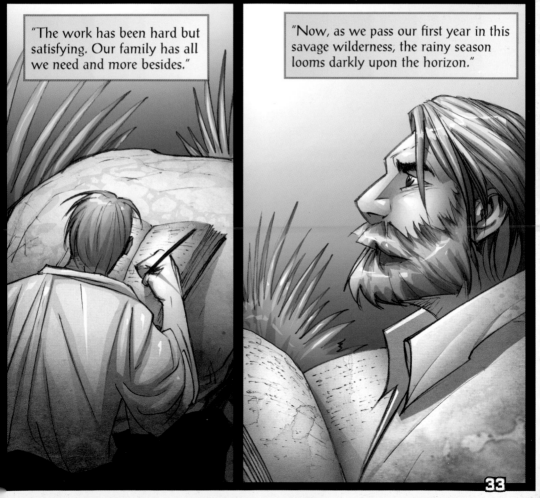

"The work has been hard but satisfying. Our family has all we need and more besides."

"Now, as we pass our first year in this savage wilderness, the rainy season looms darkly upon the horizon."

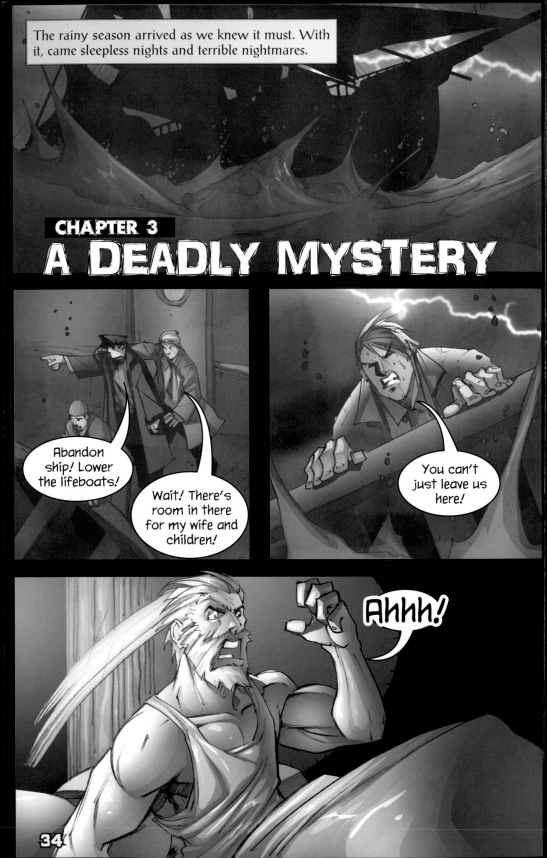

39

When we finally returned, the dark puzzle grew even more mysterious.

Thank goodness you're back!

I went in the pen to feed the animals. One of the donkeys is dead! And a pig is missing!

The boys did their best to comfort their mother, while I stayed behind to investigate.

The dead donkey didn't have a mark on him. The 200-pound pig had vanished without leaving a single track.

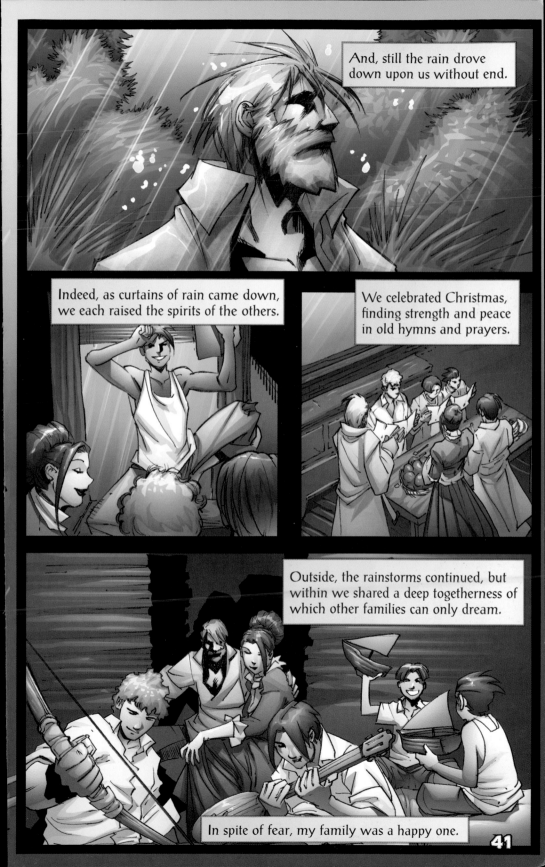

And, still the rain drove down upon us without end.

Indeed, as curtains of rain came down, we each raised the spirits of the others.

We celebrated Christmas, finding strength and peace in old hymns and prayers.

Outside, the rainstorms continued, but within we shared a deep togetherness of which other families can only dream.

In spite of fear, my family was a happy one.

Then, one day, quite by surprise . . .

Wake up, everybody! The rain has stopped!

Thank Heaven! I'd forgotten what a blue sky looks like.

Follow me!

I've been out scouting. Come see what I found!

CHAPTER 4
ISLAND OF GOOD FORTUNE

43

Soon . . .

An albatross! Looks like he's going to land in my boat!

You're exhausted, my friend.

Here, have some fresh water.

What's this? There's a message tied to your leg!

A woman? Lost on our island?!

Save a stranded woman from the smoking Rock

As he neared the volcano, Fritz heard a woman scream.

I don't understand. Where is everyone?

What is it, Turk? I've never seen him so scared.

Come on! He wants us to follow him!

CHAPTER 6
THE CAVE CREATURE

THUD!

Everyone get back!

Now, darling! The oil!

Our nameless horror, at long last, had a form. It was a gigantic boa constrictor, over forty feet in length.

Suddenly a dozen dark mysteries were made clear. Now the monster was destroyed.

We took Jenny instantly to our hearts. She was braver than anyone we'd ever known. Now, she had a new family.

And she and Fritz had each other.

Jenny brought us more good fortune only a few days later.

Are they pirates, Father?

No, not pirates.

They're searching for someone.

CHAPTER 7
RESCUED FROM PARADISE

The flag! They're flying the Union Jack! It's a British ship!

We lost little time in loading our old cannon with the last of the gunpowder and signalled back.

All of you, of course, are welcome to join us on our journey back to Europe!

Jenny and Fritz were married in London, where they continue to live happily.

Ernest, Jack, and Franz attended the best schools of Europe. Their fame grew as they told and retold the stories of our adventures.

As for us, my dear wife and I decided to remain on our island.

We realized, even through our struggles, that we'd been perfectly happy. Everything that we ever needed was already here.

In future years many others would find our island, we knew, and it would one day become a proud new Swiss colony.

For now, though, it remained ours alone. Our Eden. Our Paradise, made just for the two of us.

MORE ABOUT CASTAWAYS

Many movies, television programmes, and books, such as *Swiss Family Robinson*, tell stories of people stranded on deserted islands. But could someone really get lost at sea and survive? Below are some interesting facts about becoming a castaway.

Even with more than 6 billion people in the world, finding a place to get stranded isn't that difficult. Thousands of islands have no people at all. In fact, the country of Indonesia has more than 6,000 islands where nobody lives.

The largest uninhabited island in the world isn't small at all. Devon Island in Canada is an impressive 55,200 square kilometers. That's nearly three times the size of Wales!

Finding a place to get lost is easy, but how long could a human survive without food, water, or TV? Surprisingly, humans can last nearly a month without any food at all. In fact, magician David Blaine lasted an incredible 44 days without eating in 2003. Finding water is much more important. Experts say that more than three days without water could be deadly. And life without TV? Well, it might be painful, but it won't kill you.

If you are stranded on a deserted island, look for coconuts. These are an excellent source of both food and liquid. The husks can be used to make rope, and coconut oil can help repel pesky insects such as mosquitoes.

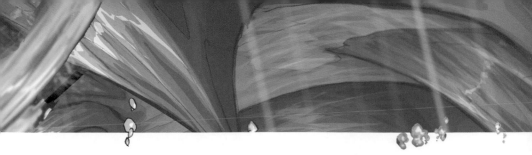

So, surviving on a deserted island is possible (at least for a while), but has anyone ever done it? Many people have lasted a few days after a shipwreck or a plane crash, but only a few can be called real-life castaways.

Perhaps the most famous castaway was a Scottish sailor named Alexander Selkirk. In September 1704, Selkirk was left stranded on a small island off the coast of Chile. With only a few tools, a musket, and a Bible, Selkirk survived alone for the next four years and four months. After he was rescued in February 1709, Selkirk wrote a book about his experience. A few years later, author Daniel Defoe turned Selkirk's story into a famous novel called *Robinson Crusoe.* This book has inspired many other adventure stories, including *Swiss Family Robinson.*

Another famous castaway, Tom Neale, wasn't stranded on a deserted island – he chose to live there! In 1952, Neale settled on a small island in the Pacific Ocean called Suwarrow. With only a few supplies, he lived by himself on the island for 15 of the next 25 years. He grew small gardens, raised chickens, caught fish, and ate coconuts. Shortly after his death in 1977, the island was declared a National Heritage Park. A small memorial on the island reads, "Tom Neale lived his dream on this island".

1. The deserted island in *Swiss Family Robinson* is filled with thousands of different types of plants and animals. Do you think all of these animals could actually live together? Why or why not?

2. Throughout the story, the family has to work together to survive on the deserted island. Which family member do you think helps out the most? Explain your answer using examples from the story.

3. At the end of the story, Mr Robinson and Mrs Robinson decide to stay on the island. Why do you think they made this decision? Would you have stayed on the island or returned home? Explain your answers.

WRITING PROMPTS

1. Make a list of five things you would want to have on a deserted island. Would you want matches, a fishing pole, or maybe your favourite book? When your list is completed, explain why you chose each item.

2. How would you get off of a deserted island? Remember, you can only use items found on the island. Explain your plan.

3. Mr Robinson and Mrs Robinson chose to stay on the island instead of returning. If you could choose to live anywhere in the world, where would you live? Explain why you would live there and what your life would be like.

Treasure Island

Jim Hawkins had no idea what he was getting into when the pirate Billy Bones showed up at the doorstep of his mother's inn. When Billy dies suddenly, Jim is left to unlock his old sea chest, which reaveals money, a journal, and a treasure map. Joined by a band of honourable men, Jim sets sail on a dangerous voyage to locate the loot on a faraway island. The violent sea is only one of the dangers they face. They soon enocunter a band of bloodthirsty pirates determined to make the treasure their own.

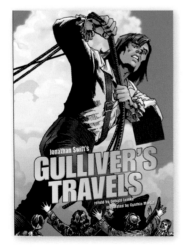

Gulliver's Travels

Lemuel Gulliver always dreamed of sailing across the seas, but he never could have imagined the places his travels would take him. On the island of Lilliput, he is captured by tiny creatures no more than six inches tall. In the country of Blefuscu, he is nearly squashed by an army of giants. His adventures could be the greatest tales ever told, if he survives long enough to tell them.

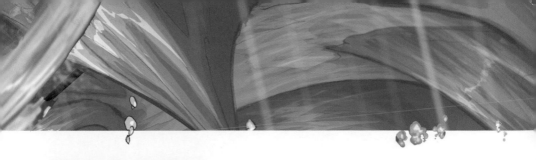

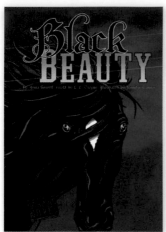

Black Beauty

Black Beauty, a handsome horse living in Victorian England, had a happy childhood growing up in the peaceful countryside. In his later years, he encounters terrible illness and a frightening stable fire. Things go from bad to worse when Black Beauty's new owners begin renting him out for profit. Black Beauty endures a life of mistreatment and disrespect in a world that shows little regard for the happiness of animals.

Journey to the Centre of the Earth

Axel Lidenbrock and his uncle find a mysterious message inside a 300-year-old book. The dusty note describes a secret passageway to the centre of the Earth! Soon they are descending deeper and deeper into the heart of a volcano. With their guide, Hans, the men discover underground rivers, oceans, strange rock formations, and prehistoric monsters. They also run into danger, which threatens to trap them below the surface forever.

GRAPHIC REVOLVE

If you have enjoyed this story, there are many more exciting tales for you to discover in the Graphic Revolve collection...

20,000 Leagues Under the Sea
The Adventures of Tom Sawyer
Alice in Wonderland
Black Beauty
Dracula
Frankenstein
Gulliver's Travels
The Hound of the Baskervilles
The Hunchback of Notre Dame
Journey to the Centre of the Earth
The Jungle Book
King Arthur and the Knights of the Round Table
The Legend of Sleepy Hollow
Robin Hood
The Strange Case of Dr Jeckyll and Mr Hyde
The Swiss Family Robinson
Treasure Island
The Wizard of Oz